THE WINTER OLYMPICS

Nick Hunter

Heinemann LIBRARY

Chicago, Illinois

Edited by Nick Hunter and Diyan Leake
Designed by Steve Mead
Original illustrations © Capstone Global Library Ltd 2014
Picture research by Ruth Blair
Production by Victoria Fitzgerald
Originated by Capstone Global Library Ltd
Printed in the United States of America in
 North Mankato, Minnesota. 122013 007920RP

ISBN: 978 1 4329 7699 6 (Hardback)
ISBN: 978 1 4329 7700 9 (Paperback)

17 16 15 14 13
10 9 8 7 6 5 4 3

Cataloging-in-Publication Data is available at the Library of
Congress web site.

Acknowledgments
We would like to thank the following for permission to reproduce
photographs: Corbis pp. 19 (© Claus Fisker/EPA), 27 (© Anastasia
Mishchenko/Demotix); Getty Images pp. 4 (Clive Rose), 5
(Cameron Spencer), 6 (IOC, Olympic Museum/Allsport), 7 (Hulton
Archive), 8 (Bob Thomas), 9 (Bongarts), 10 (Kevork Djansezian),
11 (Richard Heathcote), 12 (Jonathan Nackstrand/AFP), 13
(Alberto Pizzoli/AFP), 14 (Clive Mason), 15 (Georges Gobet/
AFP), 16 (Robyn Beck/AFP), 17 (Matthew Stockman), 18 (Bruce
Bennett), 20 (Adrian Dennis/AFP), 21 (Doug Pensinger), 22
(Jaime L. Mikle), 23 (Jamie McDonald), 25 (Clive Brunskill), 26
(Daniel Slim/AFP).

Cover photograph of Shaun White of the United States in the
finals of the men's half-pipe snowboarding competition during the
Torino 2006 Winter Olympic Games reproduced courtesy of Corbis
(© K.C. Alfred/SDU-T/ZUMA).

Contents

Some words are shown in bold, **like this**. You can find out what they mean by looking in the glossary.

Winter Wonderland

The skier has trained for four years for this moment. In a few seconds, he will plunge down the mountain at speeds of up to 85 miles (135 kilometers) per hour. In less than two minutes, if he can avoid a high-speed crash, the skier will know whether he has achieved his goal. Will he have what it takes to become the Winter Olympic champion?

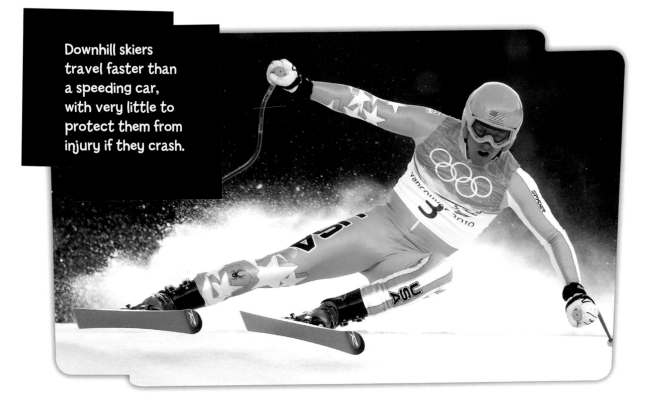

Downhill skiers travel faster than a speeding car, with very little to protect them from injury if they crash.

The Winter Olympics are the ultimate sporting event for snow and ice athletes. Every four years, thousands of skiers, skaters, and sliders test their skills against the best in the world. Often they are also testing themselves against the natural landscape and weather conditions that are the backdrop for many winter sports.

Speed, skill, and snow

The Winter Olympics include some of the world's fastest and most dangerous sports, from downhill skiing to luge. Skill and constant practice are the keys to success in figure skating and the amazing tricks of freestyle skiers and snowboarders.

THE OLYMPIC MOVEMENT

"The goal of the **Olympic Movement** is to contribute to building a peaceful and better world by educating youth through sport practiced in accordance with Olympism and its values."

From the Olympic Charter. The Winter Olympic Games, like the Summer Games, are organized by the **International Olympic Committee (IOC)** and the Olympic Movement.

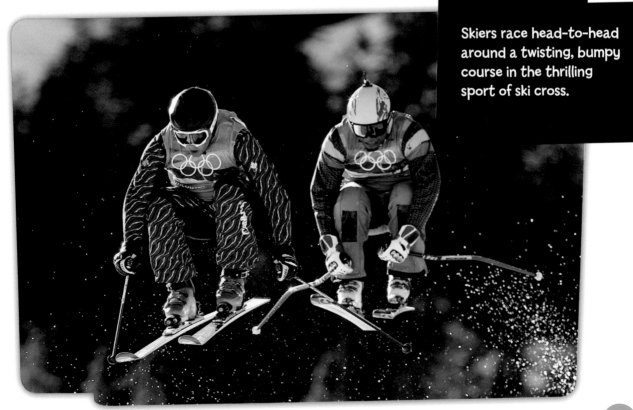

Skiers race head-to-head around a twisting, bumpy course in the thrilling sport of ski cross.

The First Winter Olympics

The first winter sporting event to take place at the Olympics was in London, England, in 1908, when figure skating was included in the Games. In 1912, Stockholm, Sweden, was the host city of the Olympics. The **IOC** tried to persuade the Swedes to stage a winter event as well. They refused, believing that winter Olympic Games would damage their own Nordic Games.

PARIS - LYON - MÉDITERRANÉE

AUX VAINQUEURS DU CONCOURS DE LA VIIIème OLYMPIADE
CHAMONIX MONT-BLANC
25 Janvier-5 Février 1924

The Chamonix Games were only officially called the first Winter Olympic Games in 1926.

OLYMPIC FACT FILE: CHAMONIX 1924

Countries: 16

Athletes: 247 men, 11 women

Most successful country: Norway

- American speed skater Charles Jewtraw became the first Winter Olympic gold medalist.
- Eleven-year-old Norwegian skater Sonja Henie failed to win a medal in Chamonix. She won three golds at later Games and went on to become a movie star.

The idea was discussed again after World War I (1914–1918), and the IOC agreed to hold a "Winter Sports Week" in Chamonix, France, in 1924. More than 10,000 spectators made the event a big success. Norway and Sweden topped the **medal table**, but Canada was unstoppable in the ice hockey competition. The Winter Olympics were here to stay.

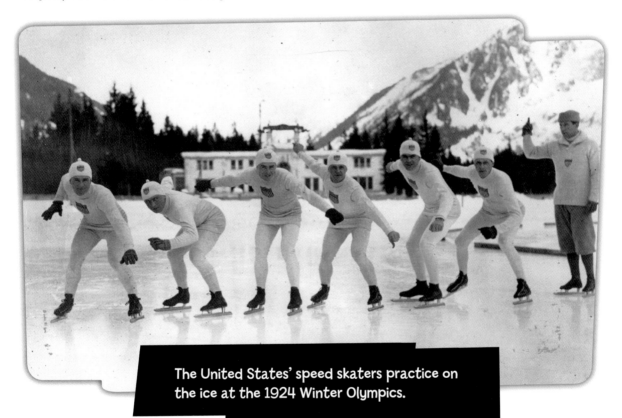

The United States' speed skaters practice on the ice at the 1924 Winter Olympics.

BOBSLED BEGINNINGS

The first bobsleds were created in the 1880s by attaching two **toboggans** together. The rules for bobsled competition were only agreed upon a few days before the Olympics started!

The Changing Winter Games

The Winter Olympics have changed constantly since 1924. By 2010, more than 2,500 athletes from 82 countries were competing at the Games. The athletes' incredible skills are now watched by a huge television audience around the world.

Ice skaters Jayne Torvill and Christopher Dean won gold at the 1984 Sarajevo Winter Olympics.

The Winter Olympics were held every four years from 1924 until 1992, except for a break during World War II (1939–1945). By 1992, the cost and effort of holding the Winter and Summer Olympics the same year was too great. The next Games in Lillehammer, Norway, were held two years later, in 1994. Since then, Winter and Summer Olympics have been two years apart.

Slippery slopes

Problems for the Winter Olympics have included too much or too little snow and ice. Only a relatively small number of countries can stage such a huge winter-sports event, but the Games have been held in Europe, North America, and Asia.

VIKING GOLD

The all-time Winter Olympics **medal table** is topped by Norway, a nation of less than five million people. Norway won the most medals at five of the first six Winter Olympics. Even in 2010, Norway won nine gold medals, equaling the United States.

Norway's Bjørn Dæhlie is the most successful Winter Olympic champion of all time. He has won 12 medals, including eight golds, in the grueling sport of cross-country skiing.

Symbols and Ceremonies

Olympic symbols are at the heart of the **Olympic Movement**. Many of these symbols refer back to the ancient Olympic Games held by the ancient Greeks from around 776 BCE. These Games were the model for the modern Olympic Games, although they never included winter sports.

Every Winter Olympic Games begins with an opening ceremony. The opening ceremony includes music and culture from the host country as well as a parade of athletes. During the opening ceremony, the Olympic flame will be lit. The flame burns throughout the Games. The Olympic flag of five interlocking rings also flies during the Games. Its five rings represent the five areas of the world competing at the Games.

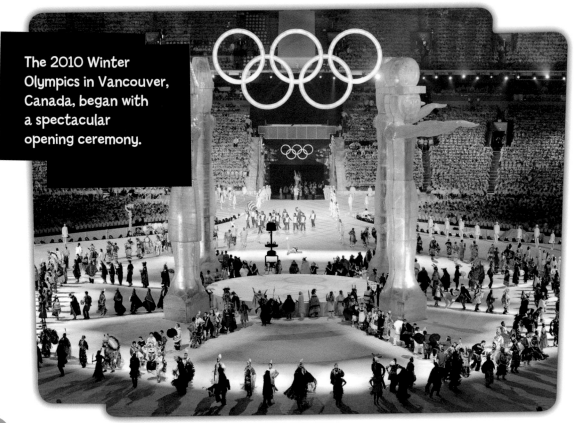

The 2010 Winter Olympics in Vancouver, Canada, began with a spectacular opening ceremony.

Torch relay

Before each Winter Olympics, an Olympic torch is lit at Olympia, in Greece. The torch is carried across the host country in a relay before it is used to light the Olympic flame at the opening ceremony. In 2010, the torch traveled 28,000 miles (45,000 kilometers) across Canada in 106 days.

OLYMPIC MASCOTS

Mascots have been part of the Winter Olympics ever since the Games in Innsbruck, Austria, in 1976. The Austrian mascot was a snowman with a traditional Austrian hat. The official mascot is often an animal from the host country. Recent Games, such as Vancouver 2010, have included several mascots to represent different features of the Games or the host country.

Ice hockey legend Wayne Gretzky lit the Olympic flame at the 2010 Opening Ceremony.

Supreme Skiers

Alpine skiing is one of the Winter Olympics' most exciting sports. The downhill champion is the fastest man or woman on two skis. Skiing is so popular, it seems amazing that the sport was not part of the Winter Olympics until 1936.

Skiers compete in downhill, super G, giant slalom, and slalom. Super G combines the electric pace of downhill with tighter turns through gates. Slalom is about keeping control all the way down the course.

Nordic skiing

Nordic cross-country skiers race over distances that are up to 31 miles (50 kilometers). They are some of the world's fittest endurance athletes.

LINDSEY VONN

American skiing star Lindsey Vonn was happier than most athletes when the downhill skiing was delayed by bad weather in Vancouver in 2010. The delay gave her time to recover from injury and ski to her first gold medal.

Sky-scraping ski jumpers are judged on style as well as how far they jump.

OLYMPIC FACT FILE: TORINO 2006

Countries: 80

Athletes: 1,548 men, 960 women

Most successful country: Germany

• Kjetil André Aamodt of Norway became the first skier to win four gold medals. He won them over the course of his 14-year Olympic career.

• Half an hour later, Croatia's Janica Kostelić became the first woman to win four golds when she won the alpine skiing event.

Going Downhill Fast

Bobsled, skeleton, and luge are sliding events. They are some of the most thrilling and dangerous sports at the Games. Teams or individuals hurtle down an icy track at high speed, steering the best line through the steep corners to finish in the fastest time.

SLED RIDES

The first bobsleds were made of wood. Today, they are made of **streamlined fiberglass** over a metal frame. This offers some protection for the athletes. The driver steers by pulling ropes attached to **runners** at the front. Luge sleds are lightweight, with no protection for athletes. Skeleton sliders hurtle down the track headfirst.

Getting a fast start is important in sliding events. Vancouver gold medalist Amy Williams was a runner before she took up the skeleton.

Vancouver tragedy

Lugers hurtle down the same track as the bobsled at speeds of around 90 miles (140 kilometers) per hour. At Vancouver in 2010, luge athlete Nodar Kumaritashvili, from the country of Georgia, paid the ultimate price for his sport. He was killed when he crashed during a practice run on the day of the Games' opening ceremony.

ICE COOL IN CALGARY

One of the most popular teams at the 1988 Calgary Winter Olympics was from a tropical island with no history of winter sports success. The Jamaican bobsled team did not challenge Switzerland for the gold medal, but it made many friends and went on to compete at several Winter Olympics.

On the Ice

Skating has been part of the Olympic Games since before the Winter Olympics even started. Individual figure skaters and pairs make intricate spins and turns look easy, but they also have to bring a lot of creativity to their routines. Any tiny mistake will be picked up by the judges.

SHORT-TRACK SMASH

Steven Bradbury of Australia was in last place in the final of the 1,000-meter short-track at the 2002 Winter Olympics when the skaters in front of him collided. Bradbury swept through to take gold.

Kim Yu-Na is one of South Korea's greatest sports heroes. She won a gold medal in figure skating at the 2010 Winter Olympics.

Super speed skaters

Speed skaters race at speeds of around 60 miles (95 kilometers) per hour. Each race features two skaters. Their skates are very different than those used by figure skaters, with longer blades helping them to go faster.

Short-track speed skating has been included at the Winter Olympics since 1992. The course is shorter, with tighter turns, and four skaters race at once. Crashes are common in this action-packed sport.

APOLO OHNO

Short-track speed skater Apolo Ohno has won more Winter Olympic medals than any other American, with two gold, two silver, and four bronze medals. In addition to shining on the ice, he also won the TV show *Dancing with the Stars* in 2007, before winning three medals at the Vancouver 2010 Games.

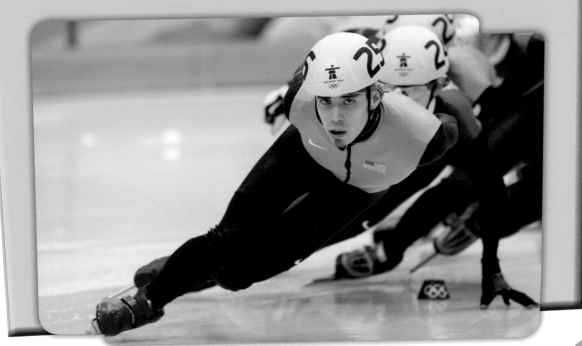

Terrific Teams

The ultimate team sport at the Winter Olympics is ice hockey. The sport has been part of the Games since the Antwerp Summer Olympics of 1920. Women's ice hockey was not added to the Olympic program until 1998, which was the same year that **professional** players in the National Hockey League (NHL) first appeared.

Events on ice have seen fierce rivalries between the United States and the **Soviet Union** during the decades after World War II, and more recently between Canada and the United States.

SIDNEY CROSBY

After receiving a string of NHL honors, Sidney Crosby's greatest Olympic moment came in 2010. He scored the goal that brought Canada victory over the United States in the final, winning the gold medal that all of Canada had hoped for.

Curlers in the house

Curling is team sport played at a slower pace. Each four-person team has to slide a large stone weighing nearly 44 pounds (20 kilograms) across the ice to an area called the house.

Curling team members brush the ice in front of the stone to help it slide farther.

Extreme Winter Sports

Winter sports have changed constantly since the Winter Olympics began in 1924. New materials and safety equipment have made sports like alpine skiing safer. They have also helped in the development of thrilling new sports, including snowboarding and freestyle skiing.

Snowboarding has become one of the most popular Olympic sports since the first competition in 1998. Athletes compete in slalom, snowboard cross, slopestyle, and the amazing **half-pipe**.

Going aerial

Freestyle skiers perform in aerials, slopestyle, half-pipe, and moguls events. In the moguls event, they must combine speed over a bumpy course with a series of tricks. The tragic death of freestyle half-pipe skier Sarah Burke in 2012 was a grim reminder that athletes often take big risks to compete at the highest level.

Shaun White

American Shaun "The Flying Tomato" White is a legend in snowboarding, with two Olympic gold medals in the half-pipe event. At the Vancouver Olympics, White performed a double McTwist 1260, a trick that only he could perform. Will he claim a third gold in 2014?

NEW TRICKS

The 2014 Winter Olympics in Sochi, Russia, will include several new events, including ski half-pipe and both ski and snowboard slopestyle. Athletes in slopestyle events will do a series of moves including grabs, grinds, and spins along a course packed with jumps and obstacles.

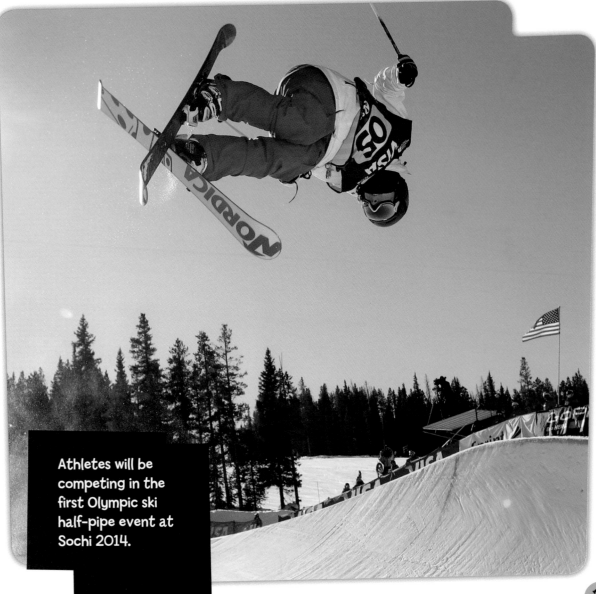

Athletes will be competing in the first Olympic ski half-pipe event at Sochi 2014.

Winter Paralympics

Hot on the heels of the Winter Olympics come the Winter **Paralympics**. The incredible athletes at these Games have each overcome a disability to compete at the highest level. The first Winter Paralympics were held in 1976. Since 1992, Paralympic athletes have shared the sporting arenas that have been used for the Winter Olympics a few weeks earlier.

Paralympic sports

Sports at the Winter Paralympics include alpine and cross-country skiing, ice sled (sledge) hockey, and wheelchair curling. The **biathlon** competition combines cross-country skiing with rifle shooting. Races in different classifications mean that athletes compete against others with similar disabilities.

Ice sled hockey is like ice hockey but, instead of skates, players use sleds to move around the ice.

Alpine skiers use different equipment. Amputees may use a single ski or **prosthetic** arms or legs. Visually impaired athletes ski with sighted skiers who guide them down the mountain.

PARALYMPIC FACT FILE: VANCOUVER 2010

Countries: 44

Athletes: 502

Most successful country: Germany

- Athletes represented more countries than ever before.
- More tickets were sold than at any previous Winter Paralympics.

LAUREN WOOLSTENCROFT

The Canadian athlete Lauren Woolstencroft was just four years old when she started skiing, despite being born missing both legs below the knee and her left arm below the elbow. In 2010, Woolstencroft won an amazing five gold medals in alpine skiing.

Controversy at the Games

Controversy is never far from the world's biggest sporting events. The Winter Olympics are no exception.

One of the biggest scandals happened before the 1994 Games, when the husband of American figure skater Tonya Harding was accused of organizing an attack on her rival, Nancy Kerrigan. Kerrigan recovered to win a silver medal at the Winter Olympics in Lillehammer, Norway, while Harding finished in eighth place.

Performance-enhancing drugs

Winter Olympic officials have to be on their guard against athletes using drugs that improve their performance. Athletes who have been caught doing this at the Winter Olympics have often been competing in endurance events such as cross-country skiing.

OLYMPIC FACT FILE: SALT LAKE CITY 2002

Countries: 77

Athletes: 1,513 men, 886 women

Most successful country: Germany

• Ten **IOC** members resigned or were expelled for accepting **bribes** in return for their votes from cities bidding for the 2002 Games.

• Athletes from 18 countries won gold, including short-track speed skater Yang Yang (A), the first Chinese Winter Olympic champion.

The Russian and Canadian pairs show off their shared gold medals at the 2002 Winter Olympics.

SKATING SCANDAL

Winning and losing in figure skating depends on the votes of judges. In 2002, the judges awarded gold to a pair of Russian skaters. Most people watching thought the Canadian pair had deserved to win. In the end, a second set of gold medals was awarded, to the Canadians. The judging system for skating was changed to prevent similar problems in the future.

Sochi 2014

Staging the Winter Olympics is a great honor and a huge project for any city. The host city is decided by members of the **IOC**. In 2014, the world's best snow and ice athletes will compete in the Winter Olympics in Sochi, Russia.

The venues for the Sochi Winter Olympics have been specially built for the Games, including skating venues and an Olympic stadium beside the Black Sea.

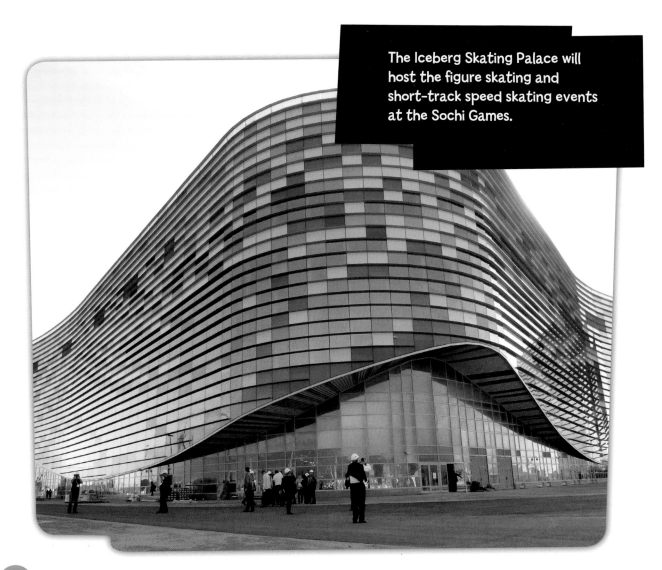

The Iceberg Skating Palace will host the figure skating and short-track speed skating events at the Sochi Games.

The world is watching

Some Winter Olympic stars will return to amaze us, and new stars will also be launched. Once again, the world's attention will be focused on the incredible Winter Olympics.

OLYMPIC FACT FILE: SOCHI 2014

- This is the first time any Olympic Games have been held in Russia. (The 1980 Summer Olympics were staged in Moscow, but Russia was part of the **Soviet Union** at the time.)
- Organizers plan to store 8.8 million cubic feet (250,000 cubic meters) of snow, just in case there is not enough natural snow. They will also use more than 400 machines to make **artificial** snow.

RUSSIA'S MASCOT TALENT

Sochi's official Olympic **mascots** are a snowboarding snow leopard, a hare, and a polar bear. They were selected by public vote on a live television show.

Winter Olympic Fact File

Winter Olympic sports

Athletes will compete in the following sports at the Sochi Winter Olympics in 2014.

Alpine skiing	**Biathlon**
Bobsled	Cross-country skiing
Curling	Figure skating
Freestyle skiing	Ice hockey
Luge	Nordic combined skiing
Short-track speed skating	Skeleton bobsled
Ski jumping	Snowboarding

Winter Olympics medal table

This **medal table** includes results from 1924 to 2010.

Country	Gold	Silver	Bronze
Norway	107	106	90
United States	87	95	71
Soviet Union (1956–1992)	87	63	67
Germany	78	78	53
Austria	55	70	76
Canada	52	45	48
Sweden	48	32	48
Switzerland	43	37	46
Finland	42	58	56
East Germany (1956–1988)	39	36	35

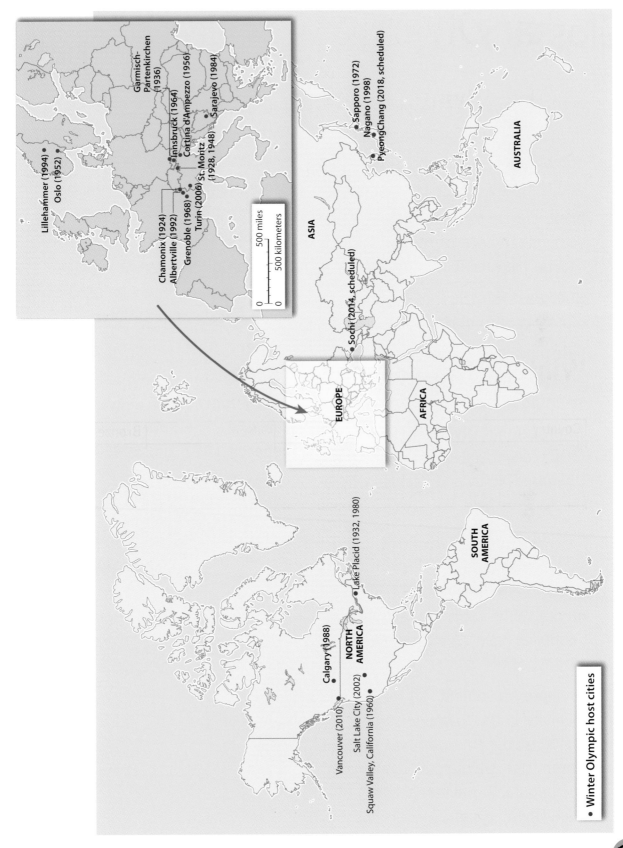

Lillehammer (1994)

Oslo (1952)

Garmisch-Partenkirchen (1936)

Innsbruck (1964)

Cortina d'Ampezzo (1956)

Sarajevo (1984)

St. Moritz (1928, 1948)

Chamonix (1924)

Albertville (1992)

Grenoble (1968)

Turin (2006)

500 miles

500 kilometers

0

EUROPE

ASIA

Sapporo (1972)

Nagano (1998)

PyeongChang (2018, scheduled)

AUSTRALIA

Sochi (2014, scheduled)

AFRICA

Lake Placid (1932, 1980)

SOUTH AMERICA

Calgary (1988)

NORTH AMERICA

Vancouver (2010)

Salt Lake City (2002)

Squaw Valley, California (1960)

• Winter Olympic host cities

Glossary

artificial made by people

biathlon winter sport that combines cross-country skiing and shooting

bribe illegal payment to someone in hope of receiving special treatment

fiberglass plastic that contains glass fibers to make it stronger

half-pipe half-moon-shaped ramp used by snowboarders and freestyle skiers to perform tricks

International Olympic Committee (IOC) organization that runs the Olympic Games and decides where they will be held

mascot animal or cartoon figure used to represent each Olympic Games

medal table table showing which countries have won the most medals at the Winter Olympics

Olympic Movement all the people involved in the Olympic Games, including the International Olympic Committee, Olympic officials from each country, and competitors of each Olympic sport

Paralympics games for athletes with a disability, held after the Olympic Games in the same place

professional someone who is paid for doing something, such as playing a sport

prosthetic device that replaces a missing arm or leg, as used by some Paralympic athletes

runners steel blades on a bobsled

Soviet Union state made up of Russia and several neighboring countries. The Soviet Union existed between 1922 and 1991.

streamlined designed to reduce air or water resistance

toboggan simple sled used as a traditional form of transportation in the Arctic

Find Out More

Books

Hunter, Nick. *Inside the Olympics*. Chicago: Raintree, 2012.

Johnson, Robin. *Ice Hockey and Curling* (Winter Olympic Sports).
   New York: Crabtree, 2010.

Thorpe, Yvonne. *Snowboarding* (Adrenaline Rush). Mankato, Minn.:
   Smart Apple Media, 2013.

Throp, Claire. *Figure Skating* (Winter Sports). Chicago: Raintree, 2014.

Web sites

www.olympic.org

The web site of the International Olympic Committee includes facts about
each Games and details of every Winter Olympic medal winner. The site also
features lots of photos and videos from Winter Olympic history.

www.paralympic.org

The International Paralympic Committee web site includes information
about the Winter Paralympics, its stars, and opportunities to take part in
disability sports.

www.shaunwhite.com

This is the official web site of Shaun White. Other Winter Olympic stars
also have web sites and social networking pages. Official sites will give the
most reliable news.

If you want to try your luck at winter sports, search for the international
and national organizations in charge of the sport. Your national Olympic
Committee will also have information about whom to contact.

Index